A Prentice Hall Guide to the Human Resource Certification Exam

Linda Howard, EdD, SPHR

Nova Southeastern University

PEARSON

Prentice
Hall

Upper Saddle River, New Jersey 07458

Editor-in-Chief: Jeff Shelstad
Acquisitions Editor: Jennifer Simon
Assistant Editor: Christine Genneken
Manager, Print Production: Christy Mahon
Production Editor & Buyer: Wanda Rockwell
Printer/Binder: Courier, Bookmart Press

10   9   8   7   6   5   4   3   2   1
ISBN 0-13-149494-5

Table of Contents

Exam Description…………………………………………...…………...1

Exam Content Outline……………………………………………....…..3

Sample Questions……………………………………...…..………..16

Practice Test……………………………………………...…..………..24

Exam Description

What is the PHR Exam?

The Professional in Human Resources (PHR) examination is a written test designed to assess knowledge of current human resources practices. The exam focuses specifically on the technical and operational aspects of human resources practices. Successful completion of the examination signifies that one has mastered the current human resources body of knowledge and thus serves a symbol of professional achievement. An individual who successfully completes the PHR examination is certified as a "Professional in Human Resources" by the Human Resources Certification Institute (HRCI), the nationally recognized Society for Human Resource Management. More information related to the examination process is available through the HRCI Website at www.hrci.org.

What is the Exam's Purpose?

Successful completion of the PHR certification exam offers:

1. Nationally recognized evidence of professional competence and achievement.

2. A credential for career advancement.

3. Recognition of professional achievement through the use of the certification designation (the letters "PHR" following one's name) on business correspondence and by displaying the PHR certificate.

Who Takes the PHR Exam?

Candidates for the exam include individuals seeking a national credential in the field of human resources, for career advancement and/or recognition of professional achievement. To be eligible for the exam, an individual must have at least two years of experience as a practitioner, consultant, educator, or researcher in the human resources field. This experience must be at the exempt level. The Human Resources Certification Institute, the national human resources credentialing body, strongly recommends that candidates for the PHR exam have at least two to four years of human resources experience at the operational level.

1

At What Point in One's Career is the Exam Taken?

Generally, the exam is taken at the early to mid-career point. Designation as a PHR at this point offers maximum benefit in terms of career advancement. However, the exam may be taken at any point in one's career, provided the eligibility requirements are met.

Exam Content Outline

The following content outline breaks down which areas are covered on the PHR exam, as well as the percentage breakdown for each area.

PHR Test Specifications

Functional Area	% PHR Exam
Strategic Management	12%
Workforce Planning and Employment	26%
Human Resource Development	15%
Compensation and Benefits	20%
Employee and Labor Relations	21%
Occupational Health, Safety and Security	6%

STRATEGIC MANAGEMENT (12%)

The processes and activities used to formulate HR objectives, practices and policies to meet the short- and long-range organizational needs and opportunities, to guide and lead the change process, and to evaluate HR's contributions to organizational effectiveness.

Responsibilities in Strategic Management

- Interpret information related to the organization's operations from internal sources, including financial/accounting, marketing, operations, information technology, and individual employees, in order to participate in strategic planning and policy making.

- Interpret information related to the general business environment, industry practices and developments, and technological developments from external sources (for example, publications, government documents, media, and trade organizations), in order to participate in strategic planning and policy making.

- Participate as a partner in the organization's strategic planning process.

- Establish strategic relationships with individuals in their organization, to influence organizational decision-making.

- Establish relationships/alliances with key individuals in the community and in professional capacities to assist in meeting the organization's strategic needs.

- Evaluate HR's contribution to organizational effectiveness, including assessment, design, implementation, and evaluation of activities with respect to strategic and organizational objectives.

- Provide direction and guidance during changes in organizational processes, operations, and culture that balances the expectations and needs of the organization, its employees, and other stakeholders (including customers).

- Develop and shape organizational policy related to the organization's management of its human resources.

- Cultivate leadership and ethical values in self and others through modeling and teaching.

- Provide information for the organizational budgeting process, including budget development and review.

- Monitor legislative environment for proposed changes in law and take appropriate action to support, modify, or stop the proposed action (for example, write to a member of Congress, provide expert testimony at a public hearing, lobby legislators).

Knowledge in Strategic Management

- Knowledge of lawmaking and administrative regulatory processes

- Knowledge of internal and external environmental scanning techniques

- Knowledge of strategic planning process and implementation

- Knowledge of organizational social responsibility (for example, welfare to work, philanthropy, alliances with community-based organizations)

- Knowledge of management functions including planning, organizing, directing and controlling

- Knowledge of techniques to sustain creativity and innovation

WORKFORCE PLANNING AND EMPLOYMENT (26%)

The processes of planning, developing, implementing, administering, and performing ongoing evaluation of recruiting, hiring, orientation, and organizational exit to ensure that the workforce will meet the organization's goals and objectives.

Responsibilities in Workforce Planning and Management

- Identify staffing requirements to meet the goals and objectives of the organization.

- Conduct job analyses to write job descriptions and develop job competencies.

- Identify and document the essential job functions for positions.

- Establish hiring criteria based on the competencies needed.

- Assess internal workforce, labor market, and recruitment agencies to determine the availability of qualified applicants.

- Identify internal and external recruitment methods and implement them within the context of the organization's goals and objectives.

- Develop strategies to market the organization to potential applicants.

- Establish selection procedures, including interviewing, testing, and reference and background checking.

- Implement selection procedures, including interviewing, testing, and reference and background checking.

- Develop and/or extend employment offers.

- Perform or administer post-offer employment activities (for example, employment agreements, completion of I-9 verification form, relocation agreements, and medical examinations.

- Facilitate and/or administer the process by which non-US citizens can legally work in the United States.

- Design, facilitate, and/or conduct the orientation process, including review of performance standards for new hires and transfers.

- Evaluate selection and employment processes for effectiveness and implement changes if indicated (for example, employee retention).

- Develop a succession planning process.

- Develop and implement the organizational exit process, including unemployment insurance claim responses.

- Develop, implement, manage, and evaluate affirmative action program(s) as may be required.

Knowledge in Workforce Planning and Management

- Knowledge of federal/state/local employment-related laws (for example, Title VII, ADA, ADEA, Vietnam Veterans, WARN) and regulations (for example, EEOC Uniform Guidelines on Employee Selection Procedures)

- Knowledge of immigration laws (for example, visas, I-9)

- Knowledge of quantitative analyses required to assess past and future staffing (for example, cost benefit analysis, costs-per-hire, selection ratios, adverse impact)

- Knowledge of recruitment methods and sources

- Knowledge of staffing alternatives (for example, telecommuting, outsourcing)

- Knowledge of planning techniques (for example, succession planning, forecasting)

- Knowledge of reliability and validity of selection tests/tools/methods

- Knowledge of use and interpretation of selection tests (for example, psychological/personality, cognitive, and motor/physical assessments)

- Knowledge of interviewing techniques

- Knowledge of relocation practices

- Knowledge of impact of compensation and benefits plans on recruitment and retention

- Knowledge of international HR and implications of international workforce for workforce planning and employment

- Knowledge of downsizing and outplacement

- Knowledge of internal workforce planning and employment policies, practices, and procedures

HUMAN RESOURCE DEVELOPMENT (15%)

The processes of ensuring that the skills, knowledge, abilities, and performance of the workforce meet the current and future organizational and individual needs through developing, implementing, and evaluating activities and programs addressing employee training and development, change and performance management, and the unique needs of particular employee groups.

Responsibilities in Human Resource Development

- Conduct needs analyses to identify and establish priorities regarding human resource development activities.

- Develop training programs.

- Implement training programs.

- Evaluate training programs.

- Develop programs to assess employees' potential for growth and development in the organization.

- Implement programs to assess employees' potential for growth and development in the organization.

- Evaluate programs to assess employees' potential for growth and development in the organization.

- Develop change management programs and activities.

- Implement change management programs and activities.

- Evaluate change management programs and activities.

- Develop performance management programs and procedures.

- Implement performance management programs and procedures.

- Evaluate performance management programs and procedures.

- Develop programs to meet the unique needs of particular employees (for example, work-family programs, diversity programs, outplacement programs, repatriation programs, and fast-track programs).

- Implement programs to meet the unique needs of particular employees (for example, work-family programs, diversity programs, outplacement programs, repatriation programs, and fast-track programs).

- Evaluate programs to meet the unique needs of particular employees (for example, work-family programs, diversity programs, outplacement programs, repatriation programs, and fast-track programs).

Knowledge in Human Resource Development
- Knowledge of applicable international, federal, state, and local laws and regulations regarding copyrights and patents

- Knowledge of human resource development theories and applications (including career development and leadership development)

- Knowledge of organizational development theories and applications

- Knowledge of training methods, programs, and techniques

- Knowledge of employee involvement strategies

- Knowledge of task/process analysis

- Knowledge of performance appraisal and performance management methods

- Knowledge of applicable international issues (for example, culture, local management approaches/practices, societal norms)

- Knowledge of instructional methods and program delivery

- Knowledge of techniques to assess HRD program effectiveness (for example, satisfaction, learning and job performance of program participants, and organizational outcomes such as turnover and productivity)

COMPENSATION AND BENEFITS (20%)

The processes of analyzing, developing, implementing, administering, and performing ongoing evaluation of a total compensation and benefits system for all employee groups consistent with human resource management goals.

Responsibilities in Compensation and Benefits

- Ensure the compliance of compensation and benefits with applicable federal, state and local laws.

- Analyze, develop, implement, and maintain compensation policies and a pay structure consistent with the organization's strategic objectives.

- Analyze and evaluate pay rates based on internal worth and external market conditions.

- Develop/select and implement a payroll system.

- Administer payroll functions.

- Evaluate compensation policies to ensure that they are positioning the organization internally and externally according to the organization's strategic objectives.

- Conduct a benefit plan needs assessment and determine/select the plans to be offered, considering the organization's strategic objectives.

- Implement and administer benefit plans.

- Evaluate benefits program to ensure that it is positioning the organization internally and externally according to the organization's strategic objectives.

- Analyze, select, implement, maintain, and administer executive compensation, stock purchase, stock options, and incentive, and bonus programs.

- Analyze, develop, select, maintain, and implement expatriate and foreign national compensation and benefit programs.

- Communicate the compensation and benefits plan and policies to the workforce.

Knowledge in Compensation and Benefits

- Knowledge of federal, state, and local compensation and benefit laws (for example, FLSA, ERISA, and COBRA)

- Knowledge of accounting practices related to compensation and benefits (for example, excess group term life, compensatory time)

- Knowledge of job evaluation methods

- Knowledge of job pricing and pay structures

- Knowledge of incentive and variable pay methods

- Knowledge of executive compensation

- Knowledge of non-cash compensation methods (for example, stock option plans)

- Knowledge of benefits needs analysis

- Knowledge of benefit plans (for example, health insurance, life insurance, pension, education, health club)

- Knowledge of international compensation laws and practices (for example, expatriate compensation, socialized medicine, mandated retirement)

EMPLOYMENT AND LABOR RELATIONS (21%)

The processes of analyzing, developing, implementing, administering, and performing ongoing evaluation of the workplace relationship between employer and employee (including the collective bargaining process and union relations), in order to maintain effective relationships and working conditions that balance the employer's needs with the employees' rights in support of the organization's strategic objectives.

Responsibilities in Employee and Labor Relations

- Ensure compliance with all applicable federal, state, and local laws and regulations.

- Develop and implement employee relations programs that will create a positive organizational culture.

- Promote, monitor, and measure the effectiveness of employee relations activities.

- Assist in establishing work rules and monitor their application and enforcement to ensure fairness and consistency (for union and non-union environments).

- Communicate and ensure understanding by employees of laws, regulations, and organizational policies.

- Resolve employee complaints filed with federal, state, and local agencies involving employment practices.

- Develop grievance and disciplinary policies and procedures to ensure fairness and consistency.

- Implement and monitor grievance and disciplinary policies and procedures to ensure fairness and consistency.

- Respond to union organizing activity.

- Participate in collective bargaining activities, including contract negotiation and administration.

Knowledge in Employee and Labor Relations

- Knowledge of applicable federal, state, and local laws affecting employment in union and non-union environments, such as anti-discrimination laws, sexual harassment, labor relations, and privacy

- Knowledge of techniques for facilitating positive employee relations (for example, small group facilitation, dispute resolution, and labor/management cooperative strategies and programs)

- Knowledge of employee involvement strategies (for example, alternate work schedules, work teams)

- Knowledge of individual employment rights issues and practices (for example, employment-at-will, negligent hiring, defamation, employees' rights to bargain collectively)

- Knowledge of workplace behavior issues/practices (for example, absenteeism, discipline)

- Knowledge of methods for assessment of employee attitudes, opinions, and satisfaction (for example, opinion surveys, attitude surveys, focus panels)

- Knowledge of unfair labor practices

- Knowledge of the collective bargaining process, strategies, and concepts

- Knowledge of public sector labor relations issues and practices

- Knowledge of expatriation and repatriation issues and practices

- Knowledge of employee and labor relations for local nationals (i.e., labor relations in other countries)

OCCUPATIONAL HEALTH, SAFETY, AND SECURITY (6%)

The processes of analyzing, developing, implementing, administering, and performing ongoing evaluation of programs, practices, and services to promote the physical and mental well-being of individuals in the workplace, and to protect individuals and the workplace from unsafe acts, unsafe working conditions, and violence.

Responsibilities in Occupational Health, Safety, and Security

- Ensure compliance with all applicable federal, state, and local workplace health and safety laws and regulations.

- Determine safety programs needed for the organization.

- Develop and/or select injury/occupational illness prevention programs.

- Implement injury/occupational illness prevention programs.

- Develop and/or select safety training and incentive programs.

- Implement safety training and incentive programs.

- Evaluate the effectiveness of safety prevention, training, and incentive programs.

- Implement workplace injury/occupational illness procedures (for example, worker's compensation, OSHA).

- Determine health and wellness programs needed for the organization.

- Develop/select, implement, and evaluate (or make available) health and wellness programs.

- Develop/select, implement, and evaluate security plans to protect the company from liability.

- Develop/select, implement, and evaluate security plans to protect employees (for example, injuries resulting from workplace violence).

- Develop/select, implement, and evaluate incident and emergency response plans (for example, natural disasters, workplace safety threats, and evaluation.)

Knowledge in Occupational Health, Safety, and Security

- Knowledge of federal, state, and local workplace health and safety laws and regulations (for example, OSHA, Drug-Free Workplace Act, ADA)

- Knowledge of workplace injury and occupational illness compensation laws and programs (for example, workers' compensation)

- Knowledge of investigation procedures of workplace safety, health, and security enforcement agencies (for example, OSHA)

- Knowledge of workplace safety risks

- Knowledge of workplace security risks (for example, theft, corporate espionage, information systems/technology, and vandalism)

- Knowledge of potential violent behavior and workplace violence condition

- Knowledge of general health and safety practices (for example, fire evaluation, HAZCOM, ergonomic evaluations)

- Knowledge of incident and emergency response plans

- Knowledge of internal investigation and surveillance techniques

- Knowledge of employee assistance programs

- Knowledge of employee wellness programs

- Knowledge of issues related to chemical use and dependency (for example, identification of symptoms, drug testing, discipline)

Sample Questions

Below are 4-5 sample questions for each of the major functional sub-areas found on the exam. The correct response is in bold.

Strategic Management

1. A company's long-term plan for how it will balance its internal strengths and weaknesses with its external opportunities and threats to maintain a competitive advantage is known as:

   a. business process re-engineering.
   b. strategic planning.
   c. job specification.
   d. competitive outsourcing.

2. A major difference between line and staff management positions in an organization is that:

   a. line managers do not have subordinates.
   b. staff manager's report to line managers.
   c. staff managers assist and advise line managers.
   d. line managers assist and advise staff managers.

3. Structural organizational change includes organizational redesign of all of the following EXCEPT:

   a. reporting relationships.
   b. span of control.
   c. departmentalization and coordination.
   d. organizational mission and values.

4. Psychologist Kurt Lewin's classic formula of "unfreezing, moving, and refreezing" is focused on which of the following aspects of organizational change:

a. dealing with resistance to change.
b. deciding which area of the organization should be changed first.
c. determining who should be in charge of the organizational change process.
d. identifying which organizational areas cannot be changed under any circumstances.

5. Six Sigma, TQM, Kaizen, and ISO 9000 are:

a. types of quality management programs.
b. various approaches to restructuring an organization.
c. performance appraisal instruments used in global organizations.
d. outdated approaches to employee training.

Workforce Planning and Employment

1. A procedure which determines the duties of various positions and the characteristics of the people who should be hired for those positions is:

a. job analysis.
b. job determination.
c. job specification.
d. job description.

2. A formula used to calculate the number of applicants that must be generated to hire the required number of new employees is:

a. job specification.
b. the recruiting yield pyramid.
c. 360 degree recruiting.
d. ISO 9000.

3. Which of the following is most likely to be a major influence on human resource management in the United States over the next five years?

a. decreasing diversity if the workforce.
b. balancing the demands of workers' jobs and families.
c. fewer women in the workforce.
d. a large surplus of well-trained younger workers.

4. The fundamental job duties of an employment position, not including marginal functions of the position, are called:

a. reasonable accommodations.
b. minimum wage requirements.
c. essential job functions.
d. job specifications.

5. Which of the following is true with regard to the use of polygraph ("lie-detector") testing in the hiring process?

a. all applicants should undergo polygraph testing to promote an honest workplace.
b. current US laws severely restrict the use of polygraph testing in the hiring process.
c. polygraph testing is a paper-and-pencil test in which an individual answers written questions about current and past dishonest behavior.
d. polygraph testing may only be used if an applicant has a prior arrest record.

Human Resource Development

1. The primary purpose of new employee orientation is to:

a. provide new employees with the basic information they need to perform their jobs satisfactorily.
b. avoid lawsuits against the company.
c. comply with Equal Employment Opportunity requirements.
d. advance the organization's strategic mission and vision.

2. Task analysis and performance analysis are useful tools to determine:

a. which employees should be hired from a given pool of applicants.
b. **employee training needs.**
c. performance appraisal ratings for individual employees.
d. the ratio between compensation and benefits.

3. With regard to evaluating employee training:

a. the most effective evaluation tool is an assessment of employee reaction to the training program, done at the conclusion of the training session.
b. calculating organizational return on investment (ROI) in training is a simple task that should be completed for all training activities.
c. there is a direct correlation between employees' enjoyment of the training experience and improved job performance.
d. **the most effective way to evaluate training is to collect job performance data before and after the training, using two groups: employees who received training and those who did not.**

4. In performance appraisal, the problem that occurs when a supervisor's rating of a subordinate on one trait biases the rating of that person on other traits is:

a. central tendency.
b. illegal discrimination
c. **the halo effect**
d. reverse discrimination

5. The process of collecting performance appraisal data on an employee from supervisors, subordinates, peers, and customers is called:

a. circular feedback.
b. **360 degree feedback.**
c. rater multiplicity.
d. inter-rater reliability.

Compensation and Benefits

1. The primary U.S. law governing minimum wage, overtime, and child labor provisions is the:

   a. Equal Pay Act.
   b. Fair Labor Standards Act.
   c. Davis-Bacon Act
   d. Employee Retirement Income Security Act.

2. A salary inequity problem, generally caused by inflation, resulting in longer term employees in a position earning less than newly hired workers in that position is known as:

   a. salary compression.
   b. job enrichment.
   c. expanded pay grade.
   d. job devaluation.

3. A job that is used to anchor the employer's pay scale and around which other jobs are arranged in order of relative worth is a(n):

   a. entry level job.
   b. benchmark job.
   c. scalable wage job.
   d. equity job.

4. In the process of establishing or reviewing pay grades, the simplest method of job evaluation is the:

   a. factor comparison method.
   b. point method.
   c. ranking method.
   d. salary data method.

5. The relationship between the value of a job and the average wage paid for that job is the:

a. **wage curve.**
b. pay grade.
c. point curve.
d. wage rate.

Employee and Labor Relations

1. Which of the following was LEAST supportive of the union movement in the U.S.?

a. The Norris-LaGuardia Act.
b. The National Labor Relations Act.
c. **The Landrum-Griffin Act.**
d. The Wagner Act.

2. In order to petition for a union election in a workplace, what percentage of employees must sign authorization cards?

a. 10%
b. **30%**
c. 50%
d. 51%

3. The process though which representatives of management and the union meet to negotiate a labor agreement is:

a. **collective bargaining.**
b. certification.
c. bargaining solicitation.
d. union organizing

4. An unauthorized strike occurring during the term of the union contract is a(n):

a. economic strike.
b. wildcat strike.
c. yellow dog strike.
d. impasse.

5. A court order compelling a party or parties either to resume or desist from a certain   action is a(n):

a. lockout.
b. boycott.
c. injunction.
d. settlement.

Occupational Health, Safety and Security

1. Under Occupational Safety and Health Administration regulations, all employers with_____ or more employees must maintain records of, and report, occupational injuries and occupational illnesses.

a. 10
b. 11
c. 50
d. 100

2. When a workplace complaint indicates imminent danger to employees, OSHA will conduct an inspection within:

a. four hours.
b. 24 hours.
c. three days
d. seven days.

3. Which of the following is TRUE with regard to OSHA?

a. Company management may not accompany an OSHA inspector during a workplace inspection.
b. **OSHA's website provides the public with details of a company's OSHA enforcement history.**
c. If employees refuse to comply with OSHA safety standards, the company is not liable for any penalties.
d. If an employee makes a complaint to OSHA, management has the right to know the employee's name.

4. The Drug-Free Workplace Act stipulates that, to be eligible for federal contracts or grants, employers must do all if the following EXCEPT:

a. publish a policy prohibiting the unlawful use of controlled substances in the workplace.
b. establish a drug-free awareness program that informs employees about the dangers of workplace drug abuse.
c. **conduct monthly random drug testing of all employees.**
d. inform employees that they are required, as a condition of employment, to report any criminal convictions for drug-related activities in the workplace.

5. The law that specifically addresses employers' responsibilities to provide reasonable accommodations to workers with chronic illness is:

a. the Occupational Safety and Health Act.
b. **the Americans with Disabilities Act.**
c. the Civil Rights Act of 1964.
d. the Age Discrimination in Employment Act.

PRACTICE TEST (200 QUESTIONS)

1. Human Resource departments serve a strategic role in most organizations because:

a. today's organizations are instituting HR practices aimed at gaining competitive advantage through their employees.
b. Human Resource departments handle downsizing and layoff processes.
c. globalization has reduced competition.
d. the workforce is becoming less diverse.

2. Human Resources departments support organizational strategy implementation in all of the following ways EXCEPT:

a. restructuring efforts.
b. instituting incentive plans, such as pay-for-performance plans.
c. developing and marketing the organization' s products and services.
d. retraining employees for redesigned work.

3. Title VII of the 1964 Civil Rights Act prohibits employment discrimination based on

a. race, color, or ethnic background.
b. race, religion, or sexual orientation.
c. race, color, religion, sex, or national origin.
d. race, gender, or religion.

4. Strategic organizational issues related to employee compensation include all of the following EXCEPT:

a. whether to emphasize seniority or performance.
b. how to handle salary compression.
c. whether employees should be paid weekly, biweekly, or monthly.
d. who should distribute pay checks to employees.

5. A specialized approach to organizational change in which the employees themselves formulate the change that is required and implement it, often with the assistance of a trained consultant, is:

a. organizational development.
b. skills training.
c. employee orientation.
d. sensitivity training.

6. Human Resource professionals need to understand the relationship between employee training and organizational strategy because:

a. training always results in improved performance.
b. HR departments are responsible for delivering employee training.
c. training is often part of managerial efforts to renew or reinvent the organization so that it can meet a strategic challenge.
d. employees generally enjoy training programs.

7. A process that aims to improve the performance and interaction within a specific group of employees is:

a. teambuilding.
b. a Scanlon plan.
c. human factors engineering.
d. survey research.

8. With regard to technology:

a. expansion of employee Internet use has had little effect on HR policies and practices.
b. most employees need little training in technology as computer usage is widespread.
c. technology and the Internet have enhanced HR's ability to deliver services to employees.
d. most organizations are decreasing, rather than increasing, technology usage.

9. Distinguishing characteristics of self-directed (self-managed) teams include all of the following EXCEPT:

a. strong managerial leadership.
b. naturally interdependent tasks.
c. enriched jobs.
d. employee empowerment.

10. Total Quality Management (TQM) programs typically include all of the following EXCEPT:

a. a focus on customer satisfaction through continuous improvement.
b. employee training designed to insure quality.
c. involvement of all members of the organization.
d. specific penalties for employees who fail to meet TQM standards.

11. HR-related guidelines for building effective self-directed teams include:

a. designating a strong leader as manager of the team.
b. eliminating cross training so that workers can concentrate on their jobs.
c. providing extensive training so that team members have the skills needed to do their jobs.
d. assigning employees who dislike teams to work together as a team to overcome their resistance.

12. Human Resources departments can make a significant contribution to business process re-engineering by:

a. strengthening the top-down communication process.
b. moving from teams to functional departments.
c. eliminating the distractions of cross-training.
d. redesigning work with a focus on multitasked, enriched, generalist work.

13. A work redesign plan whereby employees build their workday around a core of midday hours is:

a. a compressed work week.
b. job sharing.
c. a flexible work schedule.
d. telecommuting.

14. Which of the following is true with regard to flexible work arrangements?

a. Job sharing and work sharing are different terms for the same process.
b. Compressed workweeks are particularly suitable for organizations that offer services continuously, 24 hours a day.
c. Most firms using flexible work arrangements give employees broad freedom regarding the hours they work.
d. Flextime arrangements have been most successful in factory jobs.

15. A comprehensive process to determine the effectiveness of a firm's HR policies and procedures would most likely include:

a. an HR audit.
b. comparison of the firm's compensation practices with peer firms.
c. an analysis of turnover and absenteeism in the HR department.
d. a re-design of the performance appraisal process.

16. With regard to global HR management, HR practitioners should note that

a. research indicates that a significant number of employees will leave the firm within a year or two of returning home after an international assignment.
b. repatriation agreements are considered ineffective processes in today's international organizations.
c. labor strikes occur very frequently in European countries.
d. the adjustment of the employee's spouse and family to the new country is rarely a significant factor in employee performance.

17. Current global pressures that affect HR strategic management include all of the following EXCEPT:

a. employee skills deployment to the appropriate location.
b. knowledge dissemination throughout the organization.
c. identifying and developing employee talent on a global basis.
d. stressing to employees that cultures are the same around the world.

18. The management functions of most HR departments include:

a. both line and staff responsibilities.
b. staff responsibilities but not line responsibilities.
c. line responsibilities but not staff responsibilities.
d. neither line nor staff responsibilities.

19. Technological changes in the workplace have influenced the practice of HR management because:

a.   employees need less training when organizations use technology.
b.   technological changes have changed the nature of work.
c.   organizational spending on technology has reduced the funds available for HR functions.
d.   as technology advances, firms become less competitive.

20. An important workforce demographic consideration for HR professionals is that:

a. the workforce has become less diverse in recent years.
b. the average age of the labor force is declining.
c. older workers are more likely to remain in the workforce past the age of 65.
d. diversity initiatives are no longer needed in most organizations.

21. HR departments contribute a unique perspective to the organizational strategic planning process because:

a. HR offers training programs in the strategic planning process.
b. HR handles strategy implementation in regard to restructuring and organizational development.
c. HR maintains records of employee performance.
d. HR is responsible for compensation surveys.

22. Outsourcing of HR functions is a valuable organizational strategy because this strategy:

a. reduces costs.
b. increases employee commitment to the organization.
c. decreases turnover and absenteeism.
d. offers employees improved benefits packages.

23. As an organizational technology tool, HR Websites are used to:

a. provide employees with a single access point or gateway to organizational HR information.
b. allow employees to communicate with each other via electronic mail.
c. streamline the performance appraisal process.
d. minimize union organizing activity.

24. A key determinant of success in business-government employment initiatives such as a welfare-to-work program is:

a. offering salaries that are significantly higher than industry standards.
b. pre- and post-employment training initiatives, including new employee counseling and basic skills training.
c. hiring only those who speak English as their native language.
d. hiring only relatives of current employees.

25. Organizational efforts to eliminate the present effects of past discriminatory practices are collectively known as:

a. affirmative action.
b. equal employment opportunity.
c. reverse discrimination.
d. compliance strategies.

26. Which of the following actions would likely be deemed discriminatory?

a. pay differences between men and women based on seniority.
b. replacing a worker aged 45 with a worker aged 39.
c. refusing to hire women in a private for-profit business with seven employees, all male.
d. requiring disabled workers to perform the essential functions of the job for which they were hired.

27. Title VII of the Civil Rights Act of 1964 prohibits employment discrimination based on

a. race, color, religion, sex, or national origin.
b. race, religion, or gender.
c. appearance, race, color, or sex.
d. race, religion, color, sexual orientation, or gender.

28. A major provision of the Civil Rights Act of 1991 is that:

a. it limits compensatory and punitive damages for employers found liable for discriminatory practices.
b. it placed the burden of proof back on employers and permits the awarding of compensatory and punitive damages.
c. it permits the awarding of compensatory damages but not punitive damages.
d. it permits the awarding of punitive damages but not compensatory damages.

29. A basic provision of the Americans with Disabilities Act is that employers must:

a. hire disabled individuals and then lower performance standards so that the disabled will not be adversely affected by their disability.
b. make reasonable accommodation for disabled workers, even if doing so results in undue hardship to the company.
c. provide increased benefits to disabled workers, based on the extent of their disability.
d. not discriminate against individuals who can perform the essential functions of a job, with or without reasonable accommodation.

30.   The first step in the job analysis process entails:

a. deciding how the organization will use the information collected.
b. writing new job descriptions for all current employees.
c. comparing old job descriptions with new job specifications.
d. replacing job descriptions with job specifications.

31. A written statement that describes the activities and responsibilities of a job, as well as important features such as working conditions and safety hazards, is a:

a. job analysis.
b. job specification.
c. job description.
d. workforce warning and retraining notification statement.

32. The final step in a job analysis process is:

a. verify the analysis data with the worker performing the job and his or her immediate supervisor.
b. develop a job description and job specification.
c. decide how the analysis information will be used.
d. collect the job analysis data.

33. Designing job specifications based on statistical analysis:

a. is a quick, low-cost approach to the process.
b. is more defensible than a managerial judgment approach.
c. is helpful in recruitment, but not a good predictor of employee performance.
d. is illegal under Title VII of he Civil Rights Act of 1964.

34. Which of the following is true with regard to predicting organizational employment needs?

a. The most effective analysis processes examine future practices to predict present needs.
b. Computerized methods of employment forecasting are useful in small organizations but ineffective in large organizations.
c. Mathematical models such as ratio analysis examine the relationship between a causal factor (e.g., sales volume) and the number of employees needed.
d. Very few organizations engage in any kind of employment prediction process.

35. Employee requirement and availability forecasts would be most helpful in:

a. the recruiting process.
b. the performance appraisal process.
c. the employee discipline process.
d. the interviewing process.

36. Which of the following would likely be the least effective method of recruiting internal job candidates?

a. posting information on organizational bulletin boards.
b. examining HR records of current employees.
c. advertising in national newspapers and journals.
d. consulting organizational skills banks.

37. The contemporary contingent work force

a. is generally limited to clerical or maintenance staff.
b. is declining as firms continue to outsource.
c. is made up of workers who do not have permanent jobs.
d. is considered a staffing alternative of last resort.

38. In the selection process, test validity refers to:

a. the accuracy with which the test measures what it purports to measure nor fulfills the function it was designed to fill.
b. the consistency of scores obtained by the same person when retested with the same or equivalent tests.
c. the number of criteria included on the test.
d. the range of scores possible on the test.

39. With regard to Equal Employment Opportunity aspects of testing in the selection process:

a. if tests are valid, the tests need not show a relationship to job performance.
b. employers should avoid testing, as testing has been shown to violate the rights of protected classes.
c. testing always results in adverse impact.
d. employers must be able to prove the relationship between performance on the test and performance on the job.

40. An employer who wants to measure job performance directly rather than indirectly would likely use which of the following testing processes?

a. an intelligence test.
b. a test of manual dexterity.
c. a work sample test.
d. a personality test.

41. An employer who wishes to hire a recent immigrant should note the following related to U.S. immigration law:

a. a person must be a U.S. citizen, or have started the naturalization process, to be lawfully employed in the U.S.
b. employers must verify eligibility for employment prior to hiring foreign-born applicants.
c. EEOC regulations do not apply to foreign-born workers.
d. to be eligible for employment, immigrants must sign an oath of allegiance to the U.S.

42. A primary advantage of unstructured versus structured interviewing techniques is that:

a. unstructured interviews take less time.
b. in an unstructured interview, the interviewer can ask follow-up questions and pursue points of interest as they develop.
c. unstructured interviews are in compliance with EEOC regulations, whereas structured interviews are not.
d. unstructured interviews are more cost effective.

43. Which of the following types of interviews tend to be the most reliable and valid?

a. unstructured interviews.
b. structured interviews.
c. stress interviews.
d. panel interviews.

44. Factors that can undermine the usefulness of an interview include all of the following except:

a. not knowing the requirements of the job.
b. not knowing the job candidate.
c. being under pressure to hire.
d. the effect of the order in which candidates were interviewed.

45. Organizations wishing to ensure a suitable supply of employees for current and future senior or key jobs should consider implementing:

a. succession planning.
b. work-life initiatives.
c. higher compensation rates.
d. a stress interviewing process.

46. HR professionals should know the following about unemployment insurance benefits:

a. benefits are not paid unless the employee submits to an exit interview.
b. firms are required to pay benefits only for employees dismissed through no fault of their own.
c. unemployment insurance benefits are not available to exempt employees.
d. in most cases, unemployment insurance benefits expire in eight weeks.

47. The primary purpose of new employee orientation is to:

a. help the new employee feel comfortable in the organization.
b. reduce employee lawsuits.
c. provide new employees with basic information so that they can perform their jobs satisfactorily.
d. reduce turnover and absenteeism.

48. The best medium for recruiting blue-collar and entry-level workers is generally:

a. the local newspaper.
b. nationally distributed newspapers.
c. trade journals.
d. the Internet.

49. Employers may wish to utilize employment agencies in the recruiting process because:

a. it is generally less expensive to outsource recruiting than to do it in-house.
b. agencies can generally fill a particular opening more quickly than in-house HR departments.
c. agencies almost always provide higher quality candidates that those recruited by HR departments.
d. candidates, not the prospective employer, are responsible for paying the agency's fees.

50. With regard to flexible work arrangements such as compressed work week programs and flextime, HR professionals should note that:

a. flexible work schedules generally have a positive effect on employee productivity, but may increase worker fatigue.
b. in shift work, a change to 12-hour shifts from 8-hour shifts creates more confusion, since there are fewer shift changes.
c. flexible schedules are likely to increase absenteeism.
d. as programs become more flexible, they are easier to administer.

51. Which of the following job analysis methods offers the most quantifiable measures of job duties?

a. observation
b. the Position Analysis Questionnaire
c. a participant diary
d. an interview

52. Which of the following job analysis methods quantifies job duties in the three specific areas of data, people, and things?

a. the Department of Labor job analysis procedure
b. the Position Analysis Questionnaire
c. an unstructured interview
d. a participant diary

53. An advantage of job analysis methods that use quantitative measures is that:

a. HR professionals can group together, and assign similar pay to, all jobs with similar scores, even if the jobs are very different.
b. methods that use quantitative measures are much less expensive than non-quantitative methods.
c. quantitative measures never change, unlike non-quantitative measures.
d. it is much easier to plan employee training programs if quantitative measures are used.

54. HR professionals should use multiple sources of information when conducting job analysis because:

a. using only one source of information may lead to inaccurate conclusions.
b. it is less expensive to use multiple sources.
c. quantifiable information is frequently erroneous.
d. it is less time-consuming to use multiple sources.

55. With regard to writing job specifications, HR professionals should know that:

a. identifying the specifications for trained workers is much more complex than for untrained workers.
b. identifying the specifications for untrained workers is much more complex than for trained workers.
c. job specifications are not needed for trained workers.
d. job specifications are not needed for untrained workers.

56. HR professional who based job specifications on statistical analysis rather than judgment should note that:

a. basing job specifications on statistical analysis is a more defensible approach.
b. basing job specifications on judgment is a more defensible approach.
c. neither approach is defensible.
d. statistical analysis involves examination of qualitative, rather than quantitative, data.

57. Systematically moving workers from one job to another is known as:

a. job enlargement.
b. job enrichment.
c. job rotation.
d. dejobbing.

58. Which of the following would be LEAST likely used when selecting staff for assignments outside the U.S.?

a. an adaptability screening test.
b. the Overseas Assignment Inventory.
c. a test of foreign language speaking ability.
d. an occupational preferences test.

59. An HR staffing plan would likely include all of the following
EXCEPT:

a. projected turnover.
b. employee skills and quality.
c. financial resources available to the HR department.
d. an analysis of the causes of absenteeism in the organization.

60. Personnel replacement charts are primarily used for:

a. forecasting the supply of internal job candidates.
b. forecasting the supply of external job candidates.
c. writing job descriptions.
d. conducting exit interviews.

61. Which of the following tests would likely be considered the MOST
valid in terms of job relatedness?

a. a mathematics test for factory workers.
b. a manual dexterity test for insurance sales staff.
c. a typing test for medical transcriptionists.
d. a management assessment center for data processors.

62. If an employment selection test constitutes a fair sample of the duties
of the job, the test has what kind of validity?

a. content validity.
b. criterion validity.
c. construct validity.
d. position validity.

63. The process of forecasting the supply of internal job candidates would be LEAST likely to use which of the following:

a. qualifications inventories.
b. personnel replacement charts.
c. position replacement cards.
d. exit interviews.

64. A hospital that needs to recruit newly licensed physical therapists would probably be most successful by targeting its recruiting efforts toward:

a. fitness centers.
b. university physical therapy departments.
c. internal job postings.
d. local physicians.

65. Which of the following recruiting advertisements would likely be deemed in violation of EEO regulations?

a. "experienced housekeeper wanted"
b. "nursery school seeks mature child care worker"
c. "young man needed for insurance sales position"
d. "female model needed for hosiery and lingerie manufacturer"

66. In regard to employee recruiting, the term "head hunter" generally refers to:

a. candidates who are over-qualified for the job.
b. executive recruiters.
c. former employees who wish to return to the company.
d. entry-level candidates who demand large salaries.

67. Using the Internet in the recruiting process would likely be most useful when the company is attempting to recruit:

a. laborers.
b. data processors.
c. mail clerks.
d. bookkeepers.

68. The federal law that would be <u>least</u> likely to affect employment references is:

a. The Freedom of Information Act.
b. The Fair Credit Reporting Act.
c. The Family Education Rights and Privacy Act.
d. The Fair Labor Standards Act.

69. The most widely used HR selection tool is:

a. the interview.
b. cognitive testing.
c. the assessment center.
d. motor skills testing.

70. If a company wishes to measure a job candidate's stability, introversion, and motivation, it would be most likely to use which of the following selection tests:

a. intelligence tests.
b. honesty tests.
c. personality tests.
d. handwriting analysis.

71. Tests that measure traits, temperament, or disposition are examples of:

a. manual dexterity tests.
b. personality tests.
c. intelligence tests.
d. work sample tests.

72. Using a structured interviewing technique would likely achieve all of the following EXCEPT:

a. increased consistency across candidates.
b. reduced subjectivity on the part of the interviewer.
c. enhanced job relatedness.
d. more opportunity to explore areas as they arise during the interview.

73. A stress interview technique would be most appropriate for which of the following jobs?

a. an executive chef.
b. a secretary.
c. a paralegal.
d. an air traffic controller.

74. A well-designed new employee orientation program is likely to accomplish all of the following EXCEPT:

a. fewer mistakes by the new employee.
b. an appreciation of the company's core values.
c. an understanding of policies and procedures.
d. faster advancement in the organization for the new employee.

75. In order to lower the chances of lawsuits claiming discrimination in hiring, employers should note that:

a. selection tests must be related to the job.
b. it is illegal to require selection tests for protected classes.
c. selection tests need not be valid if they are reliable.
d. selection tests need not be job related as long as they are administered to all applicants.

76. Employees who are not citizens of the countries in which they are working are called:

a. expatriates.
b. home-country nationals.
c. third-country nationals.
d. naturalized citizens.

77. HR professionals can best promote transferability of training by:

a. using well-prepared speakers for training programs.
b. maximizing the similarity between the training situation and the work situation.
c. using technology in the delivery of training programs.
d. offering incentives to employees who attend training programs.

78. The most appropriate method of assessing the training needs of new employees is:

a. task analysis.
b. performance analysis.
c. cognitive analysis.
d. psychological analysis.

79. The process of verifying that there is an employee performance deficiency and determining if training is an appropriate solution is:

a. task analysis.
b. performance analysis.
c. behavioral analysis.
d. deficiency analysis.

80. Methods of determining employee training needs include all of the following EXCEPT:

a. reviewing performance appraisals.
b. analyzing customer complaints.
c. interviewing employees and supervisors.
d. examining compensation records.

81. An example of a specific performance deficiency amenable to employee training is:

a. "John has a poor attitude toward his job."
b. "Mary seems anti-social toward her co-workers in the department."
c. "Expectations for sales staff are eight new contacts per week, but Jim averages only two."
d. "Despite repeated reprimands, Jennifer just isn't working hard enough at her job."

82. In developing employee training programs, HR professionals should first:

a. distinguish between "can't do" and won't do" in terms of employee performance.
b. inventory the organization's supply of training programs to determine which program to present.
c. match the appropriate employee groups with the appropriate training program.
d. examine the organization's compensation structure to determine the cause of the performance problem.

83. Performance task analysis would likely include all of the following EXCEPT:

a. quality of the performance.
b. conditions under which the task is performed.
c. when and how often the task is performed.
d. compensation paid for performing the task.

84. The first step in the delivery of on-the-job training is:

a. demonstrate the task for the learner.
b. prepare the learner for the training.
c. ask the learner to perform the task.
d. correct the employee as needed during the performance of the task.

85. A step-by-step self-learning method that consists of presenting the information, allowing a response, and providing feedback on the response is:

a. computer based (programmed) training.
b. on-the-job training.
c. apprenticeship training.
d. simulated training.

86. The main advantage of computer-based programmed training over other training methods is that:

a. programmed training allows trainees to learn much more about the tasks to be performed.
b. it is easier to measure performance improvement with programmed training.
c. programmed training reduces training time.
d. programmed training is the least expensive training method.

87. Training programs for employees preparing for international assignments would be most likely to include:

a. task analysis training.
b. cultural differences awareness.
c. manual dexterity enhancement.
d. cognitive skills training.

88. The Human Resource department's contributions to an organizational re-engineering process would likely include all of the following EXCEPT:

a. building employee commitment for the process.
b. redesigning the organization's mission and goals.
c. redesigning work processes.
d. redesigning compensation strategies.

89. The effectiveness of an employee-training program would best be determined by:

a. measuring employee performance before and after the training was provided.
b. comments from supervisors regarding the content of the training program.
c. the number of employees who attended the training program.
d. determining employee reaction to the training program.

90. The first step in an effective performance appraisal process is to:

a. define the job being appraised.
b. measure the employee's performance on job tasks.
c. give feedback to the employee about job performance.
d. observe the employee's on the job behaviors.

91. The simplest and most widely used technique for appraising performance is:

a. the paired comparison method.
b. the graphic trait rating scale.
c. management by objectives.
d. the forced distribution method.

92. The most effective way to evaluate performance management programs is to:

a. quantify performance expectations, deliver the program, and assess differences in performance before and after the program.
b. compare the costs of such programs and select the one that is most cost-effective.
c. survey supervisors by using a questionnaire, survey, or other quantitative analysis tool.
d. survey customers for their input on employee performance improvement.

93. Organizations can promote employee involvement in the performance appraisal process by using which of the following strategies?

a. including peer performance appraisal and self-appraisal.
b. holding organizational social events, such as annual picnics.
c. basing compensation decisions on performance ratings.
d. using job enrichment for all employees.

94. A major implication of current career development approaches is that:

a. companies will need to increase spending on career development programs.
b. HR development activities serve not only the company's needs, but also the needs of individual employees.
c. companies should not provide career development programs because such programs increase turnover.
d. companies should redesign their compensation strategies to foster career development.

95. Realistic job preview strategies can enhance employee career development and help decrease turnover by:

a. informing prospective employees of the organization's compensation and benefits packages.
b. helping prospective employees decide whether the job is a good fit with their personal skills and goals.
c. explaining the organization's mission, vision, and strategic plans.
d. explaining the benefits of the organization's training programs.

96. HR professionals can most effectively identify employee training needs by conducting:

a. both task performance and performance analysis.
b. task analysis only.
c. performance analysis only.
d. neither task analysis nor performance analysis; HR professionals should rely primarily on supervisory recommendations.

97. HR management practices designed to change employee attitudes, values, and beliefs so that employees can improve the organization are collectively known as:

a. organizational development interventions.
b. employee training programs.
c. organizational reward systems.
d. management by objectives.

98. The performance appraisal method that places employees into predetermined percentages of performance categories is:

a. graphic rating scales.
b. alternation ranking.
c. forced distribution.
d. critical incident methods.

99. Which of the following performance appraisal methods is based on the supervisor's log of positive and negative employee behaviors:

a. alternation ranking.
b. forced distribution.
c. critical incidents.
d. behaviorally anchored ranking scales.

100. An effective technique to improve deficiencies in employee performance is:

a. a performance action plan that shows the employee how to improve, when improvement is expected, and how results will be evaluated.
b. a demotion confrontation to reinforce the seriousness of the performance deficiency.
c. progressive discipline to punish the employee.
d. interpersonal sensitivity training.

101. Organizational pre-retirement counseling programs would likely include all of the following EXCEPT:

a. explanation of Social Security benefits.
b. financial and investment training.
c. counseling in the area of leisure activities.
d. psychological testing.

102. Measurement of the effectiveness of an organization's outplacement counseling program would likely include:

a. employee performance appraisal records prior to the outplacement counseling.
b. the numbers or percentages of employees placed in new jobs.
c. the number of employees who were provided with outplacement counseling.
d. the size of the organizational workforce that did not receive outplacement counseling.

103. Current trends in the training and development of international employees include all of the following except:

a. increased use of technology in training and development.
b. continuing training during the duration of the international assignment.
c. significantly increased compensation for international employees.
d. increased focus on cultural awareness programs.

104. International employees would be more likely than employees working in the U. S. to receive which of the following training programs:

a. safety and security training.
b. computer skills training.
c. training in quantitative methodologies.
d. training in organizational intranets.

105. The most significant measure of the effectiveness of an employee training program involves:

a. determining if employees liked the program.
b. determining if supervisors liked the program.
c. determining if performance improvement was a result of the training or some other factor.
d. determining the training costs per employee in attendance.

106. A major consideration in the implementation of employee performance management and appraisal programs is:

a. legal defensibility.
b. the number of employees who will be appraised.
c. the size of the company's HR department.
d. the number of supervisors who will do the appraising.

107. The regulation that makes it unlawful for employers to discriminate against any individual because of race with respect to compensation or other terms of employment is the:

a. Fair Labor Standards Act.
b. the 1964 Civil Rights Act.
c. the Davis–Bacon Act.
d. the Equal Pay Act.

108. The law created to protect employees against the failure of their employer's pension plan is:

a. The Equal Pay Act.
b. ERISA.
c. COBRA.
d. The Civil Rights Act of 1964.

109. A basic principle of organizational compensation practices is that compensation should:

a. support organizational strategy by rewarding behaviors the organization values.
b. be kept lower than industry standards to increase cost savings.
c. focus primarily on seniority.
d. be kept separate from union contract issues.

110. If an organization's pay rates are similar with prevailing rates in other organizations, the compensation structure reflects:

a. internal equity.
b. external equity.
c. face validity.
d. concurrent reliability.

111. In conducting a salary survey, HR professionals would likely use all of the following EXCEPT:

a. formal written surveys.
b. telephone surveys.
c. commercial salary surveys.
d. interviews with former employees.

112. A systematic comparison done to determine the worth of one job relative to another in the organization is:

a. job analysis.
b. job evaluation.
c. a salary survey.
d. job classification.

113. The simplest method of performing job evaluation is:

a. ranking.
b. factor comparison.
c. the point method.
d. a histogram.

114. If organizational exit interviews indicate that employee turnover is due to dissatisfaction with compensation, HR professionals would likely:

a. increase pay rates immediately.
b. conduct a salary survey.
c. conduct management leadership training.
d. outsource the compensation and benefits function.

115. A collection of jobs grouped together by approximately equal difficulty levels is a:

a. pay grade.
b. pay for performance system.
c. compensation analysis factor.
d. responsibility level.

116. A wage rate that is above the rate range for its grade would result in:

a. overpayment relative to others in the same grade.
b. underpayment relative to others in the same grade.
c. grounds for termination.
d. wage compression.

117. Which of the following is an example of an executive compensation strategy that aims to increase the price of the company's stock:

a. an increase in base pay.
b. a company car.
c. stock options.
d. stock bonuses.

118. A major difference between skill-based pay and pay based on job evaluation is that:

a. skill-based pay does not consider seniority.
b. there are fewer opportunities for advancement with skill-based pay.
c. skill-based pay is based on the pay grade for the job.
d. skill-based pay tends to be lower than pay based on job evaluation.

119. Broadbanding, as a compensation strategy, is valuable for all of the following reasons EXCEPT:

a. it offers increased flexibility in compensation.
b. it supports the "boundaryless organization" concept.
c. it reduces compensation costs.
d. it supports a flatter organizational hierarchy.

120. An incentive pay plan for factory assembly line workers would be most likely to use which of the following methods?

a. Piecework.
b. Stock options.
c. Golden parachutes.
d. Perquisites.

121. Which of the following administrative positions would be considered an "exempt" position under the FLSA?

a. entry-level bookkeeper
b. word processor
c. office manager
d. clerk

122. A variable pay plan in which a corporation annually contributes shares of stock which are then distributed to employees when they retire or leave the company is known as a(n):

a. profit-sharing plan.
b. employee stock ownership plan.
c. individual stock option plan.
d. flexible benefit plan.

123. All of the following are essential to the implementation of an effective incentive plan EXCEPT:

a. units of work output must be easily measured.
b. employees must be able to exert control over the work output.
c. employees must determine the amount of the incentive per unit of work output.
d. employees must perceive a clear relationship between effort and reward.

124. A disadvantage of incentive plans such as profit-sharing, gain-sharing, and Scanlon plans is that:

a. the link between individual effort and organizational reward is not always clear.
b. such plans tend to minimize employee commitment to the organization.
c. the plans only benefit executive management.
d. most employees are not eligible to participate until they are ready to retire.

125. A major compensation consideration for expatriate workers that is NOT generally a consideration for U.S. based employees is:

a. wage compression.
b. geographical pay differentials based on cost of living.
c. decreased compensation costs for international employees.
d. the use of incentive plans.

126. A "paid time off" policy that gives each employee a total figure for annual time off including vacation, sick leave, and personal days to be used at the employee's discretion will likely result in:

a. sharply increased compensation costs.
b. increased need for temporary and part-time employees.
c. increased costs to administer the policy.
d. decreased unscheduled absences.

127. A benefit intended to augment unemployment insurance so that the employee may maintain his or her standard of living is called:

a. a Scanlon plan.
b. supplemental unemployment benefits.
c. workers' compensation.
d. a cost of living allowance.

128. The provisions of the Family and Medical Leave Act (FMLA) stipulate that:

a. workers in organizations of 250 or more employees are eligible for the leave.
b. employees may take up to four weeks leave in a 12-month period.
c. the leave may be for employee illness, or the illness of an employee's spouse or child, but not an employee's parent.
d. the leave need not be paid by the employer.

129. Methods of reducing workers' compensation costs would include all of the following EXCEPT:

a. eliminating accident-causing conditions in the workplace.
b. getting employees back on the job as quickly as possible after an injury or illness.
c. disciplining employees who file claims for workers' compensation.
d. conducting employee safety programs.

130. With regard to employee health care benefits for workers over age 65:

a. employers do not have to provide benefits to workers over age 65 because such workers are eligible for Medicare.
b. employers must provide the same health care benefits to workers over 65 as they provides to younger workers.
c. workers over age 65 are not eligible for employer health care benefits.
d. employers may include workers over age 65 in the company's health plan, but the older workers must pay the entire cost of the benefit.

131. Employees who leave an organization are generally eligible to continue their employee health care, at their own expense, for a period of up to 18 months under the provisions of:

a. COBRA.
b. ERISA.
c. FMLA.
d. FLSA.

132. As the workforce ages, more employees will likely need of which of the following benefits?

a. child care services.
b. long-term care benefits.
c. mental health benefits.
d. employer-sponsored cafeterias.

133. Employers generally favor defined contribution pension plans over defined benefit pension plans because:

a. they are easier to administer.
b. they offer retirees a guaranteed fixed sum at retirement.
c. the employees' retirement income benefits are predetermined by the employer.
d. defined benefit plans include costs for health insurance benefits.

134. An employee benefit that provides employees with counseling and/or treatment for problems such as stress or alcoholism is:

a. an employee wellness program.
b. an employee assistance program.
c. a Scanlon plan.
d. a defined benefit program.

135. Non-cash incentives provided to a company's executives are known as:

a. perquisites or "perks".
b. insider trades.
c. boardroom bonuses.
d. "platinum purses".

136. Benefits plans that allow employees to choose from a variety of benefit options are known collectively as:

a. employee assistance plans or EAPs.
b. flexible benefits plans or cafeteria plans.
c. unrestricted benefits plans.
d. health care spending accounts.

137. Groups of health care providers that contract with employers and insurance companies to deliver health care services are termed:

a. preferred provider organizations.
b. health maintenance organizations.
c. insurers of last resort.
d. fee-for-service providers.

138. The most commonly used approach to formulating an expatriate worker's pay is to equalize the employee's purchasing power across countries. This practice is known as:

a. a cost-benefit analysis.
b. a balance sheet approach.
c. an international profit and loss statement.
d. pay for performance.

139. Major considerations in the evaluation of expatriate workers' compensation plans generally includes all of the following EXCEPT :

a. evaluating the influence of the costs of living in other countries.
b. evaluating the financial incentives needed to attract and keep expatriate workers.
c. evaluating the need for repatriation procedures.
d. evaluating non-cash compensation items.

140. In considering compensation policies for expatriate workers, HR professionals should note that:

a. expatriates are generally willing to take a significant pay cut in exchange for the opportunity to live in another country.
b. expatriate employees are generally paid on a weekly basis.
c. living costs can vary widely from one county to another.
d. cost-of-living pay increases are rarely offered to expatriate workers.

141. One of the major employer advantages in contracting with health maintenance organizations (HMO's) to deliver employee health care is:

a. employees have greater choice in selecting a physician.
b. reduced costs.
c. the employer receives copies of all employee medical records.
d. premiums remain stable for a five-year period.

142. Appropriate steps employers can take to reduce employee health care costs include all of the following EXCEPT:

a. increase annual health insurance deductibles.
b. increase employee contributions to health care costs.
c. offer training programs in health and wellness.
d. terminate employees who experience significant illness or injury.

143. A salary plus incentive/commission compensation plan would be most appropriate for which of the following workers?

a. a restaurant chef.
b. an automobile salesperson.
c. a registered nurse.
d. an administrative assistant.

144. The right to purchase a specific number of company stock shares at a specific period of time for a specific price is known as a(n):

a. stock option.
b. mega-option grant.
c. optional incentive.
d. employee stock ownership plan.

145. A one-time payment made to employees terminated by their organization is known as:

a. unemployment insurance.
b. severance pay.
c. a commission.
d. employee assistance.

146. Employee benefits as a percentage of payroll are currently approximately:

a. 10% of payroll.
b. 25% of payroll
c. 40% of payroll.
d. 60% of payroll.

147. Unionization tends to be fostered by all of the following EXCEPT:

a. low employee morale.
b. employees' fear of job loss.
c. employees' lack of trust in management.
d. employers' desire to reduce organizational labor costs.

148. A form of union security in which the company may hire non-union workers, but the workers must join the union after a certain period time (if they do not, the workers can be fired) is:

a. a union shop.
b. a closed shop.
c. an open shop.
d. an agency shop.

149. The primary U.S. legislation that affirms the rights of employees to form a union and bargain collectively is the:

a. Landrum-Griffin Act.
b. Labor-Management Relations Act (Taft-Hartley Act).
c. National Labor Relations Act (Wagner Act).
d. Unionization Act of 1930.

150. In union organizing, the group of employees the union will represent is known as:

a. the bargaining unit.
b. the agency shop.
c. the representation committee.
d. the solidarity unit.

151. During union organizing activity, the following would be considered an unfair labor practice on the part of a private employer:

a. barring union organizers from soliciting employees during their work time.
b. barring union organizers from soliciting employees in a public parking lot across the street from the company property.
c. barring employees from soliciting other employees during work time.
d. barring union organizers from entering the company's executive offices.

152. The federal agency responsible for handling complaints of unfair labor practices in a union environment is:

a. the National Labor Relations Board.
b. the Office of Federal Contract Compliance.
c. the Taft-Hartley Board.
d. the National Institute for Occupational Safety and Health.

153. An employee dismissal that does not comply with the law or that does not comply with a stated or implied contractual agreement between the company and the employee is called:

a. employment-at-will.
b. wrongful discharge.
c. negligent firing.
d. defamation

154. Provisions that make it illegal for unions to require union member ship as a condition of employment are called:

a. right-to-work laws.
b. the Wagner Act, title VII.
c. collective bargaining.
d. the Walsh-Healy Act.

155. When companies resort to "bumping" and layoff procedures during a business slowdown, the determination as to which employees should be laid off is usually based on:

a. seniority.
b. committee consensus.
c. managerial discretion.
d. employee participatory decision-making.

156. Right-to-work provisions:

a. apply to all states in the U.S.
b. outlaw provisions that make union membership a condition of keeping one's job.
c. are examples of unfair labor practices.
d. are prohibited by the Taft-Hartley Act.

157. The president of the U.S. has the right to intervene in:

a. national emergency strikes.
b. wildcat strikes in manufacturing and tourism related industries.
c. economic strikes.
d. none of the above. The president may not intervene in any strikes.

158. Common reasons for the failure of an international employee assignment include all of the following EXCEPT:

a. family's inability to adjust to the international assignment.
b. employee's inability to adjust to the international assignment.
c. inability to adapt to the local culture.
d. dissatisfaction with the performance appraisal process.

159. In considering expatriate employees, HR professionals should note that:

a. labor relations practices differ from country to country.
b. strikes occur much more often in European countries than they do in the U.S.
c. grievances occur much more often in European countries than they do in the U.S.
d. unions are very rarely found in western Europe.

160. A common repatriation problem for international companies is that:

a. repatriation usually precipitates employee grievances.
b. there is usually high employee turnover following repatriation.
c. repatriated employees usually demand significantly higher salaries.
d. repatriated employees generally do not wish to return to the U.S.

161. An employee's identification with the company and agreement to the pursue the company's mission is termed:

a. the hierarchy of needs.
b. employment-at-will.
c. employee commitment.
d. employee assistance.

161. HR professionals can make a significant contribution to improved employee relations and a positive organizational culture by:

a. serving as a linkage between employees and management during periods of organizational change.
b. distributing copies of the Worker Notification and Retraining Adjustment Act so as to improve organizational communication.
c. dismissing employee grievances as counterproductive to organizational functioning.
d. initiating frequent restructuring initiatives.

163. HR efforts to create positive employee relations can be hindered by:

a. negative managerial and supervisory philosophies.
b. federal and state workplace laws.
c. the size of the company.
d. location of the company.

164. Activities to encourage employee organizational commitment include all of the following EXCEPT:

a. promote fair treatment.
b. establish the value that people are important in the organization.
d. encourage employees to develop to their full potential.
e. abolish union activity.

165. Charges of unfair labor practices are filed with the:

a. court of appeals in the location in which the company is headquartered.
b. National Labor Relations Board.
c. local police.
d. National Guard.

166. If an employee files an unfair labor practice charge against a company:

a. the company can file a grievance against the employee.
b. the company may not discriminate against the employee simply because of the filing.
c. employers may decertify the union.
d. the employee can be demoted, but not fired.

167. Which of the following is FALSE with regard to unions?

a. After a bargaining unit is established, employers may refuse to bargain with the union.
b. In the U.S., union membership has experienced an overall decline since the 1950's.
c. Wages of union members are usually higher than those of nonunion members in the same industries.
d. Union workers generally enjoy better benefits packages than do non-union workers.

168. Collective bargaining requires that union and management negotiate in all of the following areas EXCEPT:

a. wages.
b. hours of work.
c. conditions of employment.
d. stock options offered to management.

169. The most time-consuming strategy in negotiating a union contract is usually:

a. the preparation phase prior to the negotiation.
b. the examination of the current labor contract.
c. the negotiation meeting.
d. notifying employees that the contract has been ratified.

170. All of the following are acceptable collective bargaining items EXCEPT:

a. wages of hourly workers.
b. the number of sick days employees may take in a given year.
c. the number of paid holidays offered by the company.
d. the qualifications of members of the company's board of directors.

171. A female manager who requires a male employee to go on a date with her in order for the employee to be considered for a promotion:

a. may be engaging in quid pro quo sexual harassment.
b. is not engaging in unacceptable behavior, as only male employees can be found guilty of sexual harassment.
c. may do so only in a union environment.
d. is probably just joking, in an attempt to improve workplace relationships.

172. A "decision-making leave" may be offered to employees as part of:

a. the Family and Medical Leave Act.
b. the Walsh-Healy Act.
c. an HMO health benefits package.
d. an employee discipline process.

173. An employee discipline process that emphasizes harsher penalties for repeated infractions is called:

a. progressive discipline.
b. employment-at-will.
c. dismissal and termination.
d. escalation of force.

174. "Reasonable accommodation" by employers is specifically required by:

a. most progressive discipline policies.
b. the Age Discrimination in Employment Act.
c. the Americans with Disabilities Act.
d. random drug testing policies.

175. Of the following grounds for dismissal, which would likely be most difficult to prove?

a. insubordination.
b. stealing.
c. chronic absenteeism.
d. poor quality work.

176. A more positive workplace can be created if managers and supervisors communicate to employees exactly what their jobs require in terms of performance. This kind of communication is called:

a. employee engagement.
b. expectation clarity.
c. the discipline process.
d. an exit survey.

177. A commonly used method of measuring employees' perceptions of fair treatment is:

a. an employee opinion survey.
b. an examination of employee dismissal records.
c. examining utilization records of employee assistance programs.
d. examining absenteeism rates.

178. A major indicator of management commitment to fair treatment in the workplace is:

a. the degree to which employees feel they are able to participate in decisions that affect them.
b. the frequency of employee social activities in the workplace.
c. the size of the workforce.
d. the frequency of performance appraisal.

179. Prior to beginning an employee discipline process, HR professionals should encourage managers to:

a. give the employee a written warning.
b. make sure the evidence supports the charge of wrongdoing.
c. give the employee a verbal warning.
d. conduct a formal employee performance appraisal.

180. A conflict resolution technique in which a neutral third party attempts to assist the conflicting parties in reaching an agreement is:

a. mediation.
b. cooperation.
c. arbitration.
d. dissolution.

181. The conflict resolution technique which guarantees a solution to an impasse by dictating the terms of the settlement is:

a. mediation.
b. arbitration.
c. conciliation,
d. grievance hearing.

182. An example of management failure to bargain in good faith with a union is:

a. bypassing the union representative.
b. refusing to allow a closed shop.
c. demanding that the two parties discuss severance pay.
d. proposing drug testing of employees.

183. The union decertification process is:

a. essentially similar to the union certification process in terms of steps in the process
b. similar to the union certification process, except that a higher percentage of votes is needed to decertify the union that was needed to certify the union.
c. a complex and very expensive process that usually results in failure.
d. currently illegal under the Wagner Act.

184. An appropriate action for employers attempting to avoid unionization would be to:

a. threaten employees with loss of their jobs if they unionize.
b. provide supervisory training regarding unfair labor practices and management effectiveness/leadership training.
c. decrease compensation as a punishment for union organizing activity.
d. initiate small but strategic layoffs.

185. In general, employees who feel they are treated fairly will:

a. be more likely to unionize.
b. have lower retention rates.
c. be more productive.
d. have higher absence rates.

186. Employees of hostile or abusive supervisors are more likely than other employees to do all of the following EXCEPT:

a. report high stress levels.
b. quit their jobs.
c. report lower satisfaction with life.
d. participate in employee training programs.

187. A appropriate technique HR professionals can use to increase employee involvement in workplace improvement initiatives is to:

a. foster an atmosphere of open communications and invite employee input.
b. create employee discipline guidelines for those who do not participate.
c. enlarge the jobs of those who refuse to participate in involvement activities.
d. involve only managers and supervisors in workplace improvement initiatives.

188. Managers who need to disseminate specific information quickly throughout the organization should use which of the following communication approaches?

a. Top-down communication.
b. Bottom-up communication.
c. Quality circles.
d. Employee participatory management.

189. An abnormal health condition caused by exposure to environmental factors associated with employment is a(n):

a. occupational illness.
b. repetitive stress injury.
c. health citation.
d. malingering.

190. The federal law that most specifically and comprehensively addresses workplace health and safety is:

a. OSHA.
b. ADA.
c. COBRA.
d. ERISA.

191. If an employee is injured at work, the most appropriate initial action would be to:

a. provide first aid followed by medical attention.
b. notify the company's legal defense team.
c. notify OSHA.
d. consult the employee's benefits package to determine health coverage.

192. Identification of employee alcohol abuse:

a. is often difficult, as symptoms such as tardiness can occur with other kinds of behavior problems as well as alcohol abuse.
b. should be done routinely with blood alcohol screenings.
c. should be grounds for immediate dismissal.
d. should trigger a formal disciplinary proceeding.

193. The federal legislation that pertains to workers with chronic illness such as asthma or diabetes is:

a. the Americans with Disabilities Act.
b. the Age Discrimination in Employment Act.
c. Title VII of the 1964 Civil Rights Act.
d. the Equal Pay Act.

194. Positive steps employers can take to reduce workplace violence include all of the following
EXCEPT:

a. providing workplace safety and security training.
b. creating an organizational culture that emphasizes mutual respect.
c. refusing to hire employees who have ever been convicted of any type of violent act.
d. providing security staff to monitor the workplace.

195. If an OSHA inspector shows up at the workplace, the first step an HR professional should take is:

a. check and verify the inspector's credentials.
b. close the workplace and send the employees home.
c. deny any violation noted by the inspector.
d. secure all health and safety related company records in a locked location.

196. A major concern in the area of occupational injury is:

a. employee nutrition.
b. repetitive stress injuries due to cumulative trauma.
c. anorexia among female employees.
d. skin diseases due to handling computer equipment.

197. An organization that employs many workers who smoke cigarettes should note all of the following EXCEPT:

a. smokers have higher absenteeism rates that nonsmokers.
b. organizations that have significant numbers of smokers generally pay higher health and fire insurance premiums.
c. instituting a ban on hiring smokers is generally illegal under federal law.
d. smokers have greater risks for occupational accidents than nonsmokers.

198. A special health and safety concern for expatriate employees, more so than those in the U.S., is:

a. possible security threats in foreign countries.
b. asbestos exposure.
c. cigarette smoking.
d. alcohol abuse.

199. HR professionals who work in fast paced organizations should to all of the following EXCEPT:

a. monitor employees for signs of stress and burnout.
b. provide training programs in burnout prevention.
c. try to give employees more control over their jobs.
d. report employees who seek help with stress-related problems to their supervisors.

200. Employers who reward employees for increasing the number of days without a workplace injury:

a. will likely have a safer workplace.
b. may not do so without union approval if the company is unionized.
c. are governed by the provisions of OSHA.
d. must communicate reward policies in writing.

To view the correct answer key for your Practice Test, please visit the student side of the Companion Website which corresponds to your textbook:

DESSLER, *HUMAN RESOURCE MANAGEMENT, 10TH EDITION*

www.prenhall.com/dessler

GOMEZ-MEJIA, BALKIN, AND CARDY, *MANAGING HUMAN RESOURCES, 4TH EDITION*

www.prenhall.com/gomez

MONDY, NOE, AND PREMEAUX, *HUMAN RESOURCE MANAGEMENT, 9TH EDITION*

www.prenhall.com/mondy